The American Disability Act and Websites

SCOTT WHITEHEAD

Copyright © 2017 Scott Whitehead

All rights reserved.

ISBN-13:
978-1542560856

ISBN-10:
1542560853

CONTENTS

Chapter	Title	Page
1	About The American Disability Act and Websites	1
2	Why Comply To WCAG 2.0 Accessibility	4
3	Why ADA Legislation for the Disabled is So Important	8
4	Website Accessibility for Section 508	13
5	The Process of How and Why to Report Businesses That Infringe The Law	17
6	What is Web Accessibility for Websites?	22
7	ADA Compliance and How it Affects Web Designers	27
8	How and Why You Should Test Your Website for ADA Compliance	30
9	What is Required to Ensure a Website is ADA Compliant	34
10	ADA Compliance Testing and It's Importance	37
11	Why It's So Important if you Run a Business	40
12	ADA Compliance and How it Effects Your Charity and Charitable Business	44
13	Section 508 Compliance Examples With Fixes Conclusions	47 50
	References	52
	About The Author	56

Chapter 1

About the American Disability Act and Websites

A lot of people are still clueless about the American Disability Act or ADA. Business owners - in particular - need to familiarize themselves about ADA in order to comply with its rules and regulations. So, what is the American Disability Act?

The ADA is a far-reaching piece of legislation in the United States, that was first signed in 1990. Its goal is to limit its discriminatory practices towards people with disabilities. The act and the amendments made over the years have provided equal opportunity for individuals with disabilities, whether it was in employments, public accommodations, transportation, commercial facilities, and local and state government services. Both private and public organizations are affected by the ADA.

Before the boom of the internet, it was assumed that ADA only applied to physical structures. However, the act doesn't specify whether it only applies to brick and mortar locations and that's why it was open to interpretation. After several lawsuits filed against companies for inaccessible web services and websites, it was ruled that the ADA also applies to the internet. Keep in mind that the ruling is **not** consistent across all jurisdictions.

ADA Compliance and Websites

Title III of the ADA requires businesses to ensure that individuals with disabilities also have access to the same services as people who are not disabled. This includes websites and digital media. While the American Disability Act only applies to businesses with 15 or more employees, small businesses can also reap the benefits of making their website ADA compliant. Web developers should also consider ADA compliance and websites admins must ensure that all pages are accessible to everyone.

What is the American Disability Act? And It's Effect on Websites

A public website has to be accessible to everyone. In the past, only federal and state websites are required to comply with the Section 508 of the American Disability Act.

ADA Effect on Websites

The World Wide Web Consortium and the Web Accessibility Initiative have created the Web Content Accessibility Guidelines or WCAG. The standards are continuously updated through time, and the current version, WCAG 2.0 AA has become an ISO International Standard for the web. (1) WCAG 2.0 is expected to be added as part of Section 508 guidelines in the near future.

Businesses need to ensure that their websites are ADA compliant. That way they are more able to avoid lawsuits. Therefore businesses must ensure that their web designers are aware of ADA compliance and websites can be access by everyone, with or without disabilities.

Chapter 2

Why Comply To WCAG 2.0 Accessibility

Having a public access website now means that you have to be accessible to all users, even if you are not a government organization. In the past, only government and federal websites needed to be in compliant with Section 508. Section 508 includes a set of rules and regulations that websites need to follow to make them accessible to those with disabilities. The update in 2001 was based on the WCAG 1.0. However, WCAG 2.0 Accessibility will be added to Section 508 guidelines in the near future. (2). WCAG 2.0 Accessibility guidelines have already been adopted in Canada, and other countries have their own similar guidelines.

What is the American Disability Act? And It's Effect on Websites

What Can Happen Without WCAG 2.0 Accessibility

With these new website guidelines being put into place, the question then becomes "what happens if you are not compliant with the guidelines?" The simple answer is you can end up in a court of law, which has been happening more in the last few years than ever before.

One of the biggest and most recent cases was against the H&R Block Corporation. The reason for this court case was based on the fact their websites were not accessible to the blind. This was one of the first cases where a company was sued because they did not meet ADA requirements, it also maybe the first time that a website was stated to be a place of public accommodation (3).

However, this was not the first time a website was asked to follow the Website Accessibility Guide. Monster.Com, which is one of the largest job search websites, signed an agreement to create a new web accessibility program by National Federation of the Blind, and the Attorney General's.

More companies may be asked to do this in the future (4).

One of the most famous cases was in 2008 and involves the NFB and the Target Corporation (3). The result of this case was a settlement of $6 million dollars to the California NFB. Target also agreed to work with the NFB to certify their website with the NFB's Non-Visual Accessibility Web Certification Programs.

The Extent of The Risk

While many of the cases have been settled outside of court, there is no of knowing how many websites have been threatened with lawsuits. Avoiding these lawsuits about how accessible a website is started by using the Website Accessibility Checklist at http://compliant.website/wcag-2-0-accessibility-guide-checklist/. The checklist on this web page describes the basic needs of a website to ensure it is seen as accessible (5).

What is the American Disability Act? And It's Effect on Websites

Another method to check how accessible your website is to have a website audit; which is more thorough checks much more than what is on the Website accessibility checklist. An audit checks the whole website and recommends what changes should be done to the website to make it accessible. Since many guidelines are changing, and lawsuits starting to clarify what websites need to have, the work needs to be done now. (6)

Chapter 3

Why ADA Legislation for the Disabled Is So Important

People with disabilities have faced a wide range of discriminations ranging from outright exclusion, relegation to much lesser services, along with the discriminatory impacts of transportation, communication, and architectural barriers among many other instances. The ADA legislation for the disabled was founded on the idea that with the correct support and assistive technologies, people with disabilities can still contribute to growing the nation's economy. (7)

What is ADA?

The American with Disabilities Act (ADA) ensures that everyone living with disabilities has a greater chance to live a thriving life of equality and freedom. It was signed into law on July 26, 1990 when it passed Congress with a tremendous bi-partisan support.

What is the American Disability Act? And It's Effect on Websites

Ever since it was first signed, the ADA legislation for the disabled has helped protect those with disabilities in various aspects ranging from employment to accessing various public services, like transportation and access to establishments. (7)

Why is ADA Important?

Today, there are more than 54 million people in America who have a type of disability. That amounts to almost one person in every group of five residents. This number is not static, and it still continues growing as more people get disabilities, commonly through ageing, coming into harm by accident, as well as health defects from disease. The ADA assistance for people with disabilities ensures that the rights of these people are not compromised. (8)

Like other civil right laws, the ADA legislation for the disable is all about ensuring equal opportunity.

The law makes it very clear that the equal treatment of people with disabilities is not necessarily identical treatment. (9) For instance, letting all employees have identical opportunities to use restrooms located up one flight of stairs would be equal treatment, but would be not be a practical benefit and would indeed be a hindrance for wheelchair bound employees, alternative access would be required.

ADA and Websites

The Department of Justice, which is the enforcer of ADA, has clearly stated that Title III of the ADA legislation for the disabled is also applicable to website accessibility. (10) Even as the specifics of ADA and websites are still being ironed out in proposed amendments, actions to enforce these laws are currently ongoing.

Title III claims have increased by 40% as the DOJ continues to receive accessibility complaints. (11)

What is the American Disability Act? And It's Effect on Websites

This has resulted in numerous lawsuits and fines for infringements as disabled people seek the rights, especially with regards to modifying websites according to the WCAG 2.0 AA Guidelines.

It's easy to see what the attraction is for these lawsuits;

1. For disabled users its clear and easy to identify and explain the problems they face when using these websites
2. For attorneys it's easy to identify and collate the necessary information to make a case through the courts.
3. For attorneys seeking to defend their clients, its costly and complex to refute the claims and may require technical expert witness services to work on the defense.

Conclusion

The ADA legislation for the disabled enables any discriminated person with disability to easily file a claim whenever they feel they have been discriminated against. Organizations and companies have a responsibility to ensuring they create an equal environment to those with disabilities, or suffer the consequences of legal action that can lead to damages and fines. The action organizations need to take to ensure compliance includes making websites more accessible, especially as many public services are available online nowadays.

Chapter 4

Website Accessibility for Section 508

Section 508 is a set standard that requires all federal agencies to provide software and have website accessibility to people with disabilities. (12) Even if your business is not one of the federal agencies that are required to be in compliance with Section 508, building a website that is compliant ensures your website more accessible to everyone.

At the moment, many websites built do not comply and there is no available technology to easily make all compliant. Depending on the size and function of the website in question, the process of improving website accessibility is a long and complex one; however, it is becoming more and more important to address, and every day it is not addressed is another day of risk of legal action being taken against your organization.

Here are some of the first steps you need to take if you want to improve accessibility to your organizations' website.

The First Step to Website Accessibility

The first step to making your website more accessible is to figure out if you need to be in compliance with Section 508. If your business or organization is required by federal law to comply with Section 508, you will mostly likely have a federal coordinator for your business. If you are not required to comply with Section 508, the process can take longer, and you also have the choice of what areas you will want to address first. You should create a list of what you believe should be updated first, and work on those items.

Thankfully when you are looking to improve your website accessibility, there are several well established and recommended online resources that can help you with the process. W3C Web Accessibility Initiative has guidelines about international standards of website accessibility.

What is the American Disability Act? And It's Effect on Websites

They also have a very useful before and after tool that shows the elements that make a website accessible, load your web page and it will identify the errors and show what the page will look like after the errors are corrected.

Tools you can use include:

- http://www.508checker.com/
- http://monsido.com/
- https://tenon.io/

Once you have an idea of what changes you need to make to a website to ensure it is more accessible, the next step is to take a really close look at your business/organization's website. Most of the time, there are simple design changes that can help your website's accessibility. For example using green on a red background would cause problems for people who are colorblind.

For some projects changes will be as minor as that, however for some websites a complete overhaul may be necessary.

There are testers available that you can use to find out how accessible your website is and what you need to do, and it is advisable to employ such a tester before starting the new site to ensure ADA compliance is pertinent to the brief from start to finish.

Section 508 VPATS

In some cases, the use of software can help with your website accessibility. Many websites that comply with Section 508 use VPAT, or Voluntary Product Accessibility Template, to ensure full compliance. (14) A VPAT is a document that fully explains how accessible the software needs to be. While VPAT was created for the government to compare vendors, private businesses are also allowed to use it to find the best option of programs for their business. Building a website that is Section 508 compliant takes a lot of work. Most of the websites that follow all the guidelines are usually built from the ground up. However, adding some basic features to your website can make it more accessible to all users.

Chapter 5

The Process of How and Why to Report Businesses That Infringe the Law

The internet has truly become an incredibly important part of our lives; which is why it's particularly important for businesses with websites to abide by the current state legislation. Websites are the faces of business online, ecommerce sites for example are, by definition, paramount for the overall operation of the company on the internet. This is the main reason for which they are strictly regulated in order to be equally accessible to all people, just like any conventional business. When you notice that a website isn't ADA Compliant, you are capable of reporting it and even get compensation in certain situations.

Reporting websites that are not user friendly might seem like something easy, but there are quite a few things that you need to account for. So, let's take a closer look.

How Can You File an ADA Complaint?

The first thing that you need to understand is that if you or another person has been thoroughly discriminated against by a particular entity which is known to be covered by the ADA, you are capable of filing a complaint. You need to file it with the DRS (Disability Rights Section) in the DOJ (Department of Justice). You can submit this particular complaint through the Internet, by mail or you can fax it. To learn more about filing an ADA complaint, visit www.ada.gov/filing_complaint.htm. To file an ADA complaint you may send the information requested at www.ada.gov/fact_on_complaint.htm to:

US Department of Justice 950 Pennsylvania Avenue, NW

Civil Rights Division

Disability Rights Section 1425 NYAV

Washington, D.C. 20530

Fax: (202) 307-1197

What is the American Disability Act? And It's Effect on Websites

You may also file a complaint online at

www.ada.gov/complaint/

Or call:

ADA Information Line: 800-514-0301 (voice) or 800-514-0383 (TTY).

Main Section Telephone Number: 202-307-0663 (voice and TTY) (15)

The Information Required

Of course, you need to know that reporting non-compliant websites require you to pinpoint certain information. You need to state your own credentials as well as the name and address of the business/organization for which you believe has committed this particular act of discrimination. Pinpointing the exact website is particularly important.

The DOJ also expects you to briefly describe the acts of discrimination and any other information that you may find relevant. You need to leave information for further contact and when you file the complaint.

What Happens Next?

As per the state's legislation, every complaint filed to the ADA is opened for processing and review. There are a few possible options which are based on the overall decision taken by the DOJ. Once you have filed a complaint, you may be;

- contacted for additional information,
- referred to the ADA Mediation program
- referred to the attorney's office for investigation
- passed to another federal agency which is responsible for the types of the problems you've addressed,

and the DOJ can begin investigating or consider the claim for litigation.

What is the American Disability Act? And It's Effect on Websites

As you can see, there are different possibilities which will depend on the type of issues that you've raised while reporting non-compliant websites. (15) You can also initiate a procedure for getting compensation for ADA non-compliant websites, in the event in which you've incurred certain damages.

Chapter 6
What is Web Accessibility for Websites?

There is a common fallacy about the term "web accessibility". The term is usually associated directly and exclusively with people suffering from disability and the distinct environment, whereas in terms of building a website they commonly refer to it as providing the people with disability with access to the web. This is not entirely wrong but more of an incomplete definition.

Web accessibility definition

Web accessibility is beyond the mere providing of access to people who have noticeable deficiency such as those people with visual impairment; it is giving a fair access to every individual of different places regardless of the condition, age, health, gender, and race. (16)

What is the American Disability Act? And It's Effect on Websites

Being in Compliant with Section 508; Websites

When we are talking about web accessibility, we will often encounter two prevailing terms; Section 508 and the WCAG 2.0.

There are many general usability guidelines that make content more usable by all people, including those with disabilities. However, WCAG 2.0 only includes those guidelines that address problems particular to people with disabilities. This includes issues that block access or interfere with access to the Web more severely for people with disabilities.

WCAG 2.0 states that the content of the website should be robust, understandable, operable and perceivable. "If any of these are not true, users with disabilities will not be able to use the Web." (22)

The Rehabilitation Act of 1973 where the Section 508 websites is included highly prevents the discrimination under the basis of deficiency.

It highly instructs the agencies to provide an access to the disabled person which is comparable to the access of a normal person. Moreover, the deadlines for these changes to be made have all passed, that is to say that for over a decade the Section 508 laws have been in place and requirements for compliance explained and given to be upheld. (13)
One importance of turning your site into a Section 508

Website is the fact that you will be able to understand the

behavior and online activity of people with impairment.

Based on the statistics released by the World Health

Organization, around 285 million individuals all over the

world have visual impairment. (16) There is a strong

business case for focusing on addressing compliance for the

ability to attract new business and repeat business.

These people have the ability to access the web using tools

such as keyboard navigation and screen readers.

What is the American Disability Act? And It's Effect on Websites

Those who have mild disability such as low vision will highly rely on higher contrast, vivid colors and maximizing the screen size.

One of the biggest challenges in creating a Section 508 websites would be the technology. First, is due to the browser choice; IE or Internet explorer is one of the widely used browsers all over the world, but web designers and coders regularly report that it is also one of the least accommodating. Traffic from other browsers normally make up a lot of the traffic.(17) Normally, you will have to provide that percentage with the same level of experience. One of the best ways to do this is to perform cross-analysis of browser.

There are ways to improve Section 508 websites using semantic HTML for the blind users. Semantic HTML will definitely help them to navigate freely on the different sections of the website, fill out online forms and navigate on a more complex behavior.

When it comes to the deaf user, you have to understand that most of them have the difficulty in processing the text. They will also find it hard to understand audio or video file; which is why you need to incorporate subtitles, closed caption subtitles and transcriptions. Web accessibility also affects dyslexic and autistic users. See to it that you will provide graphic representation for the dyslexic users and create a concise and simple text for individuals with autism.

Always remember that web accessibility is something that should be conducted and evaluated by a human, though an automated tool may provide some assistance.

What is the American Disability Act? And It's Effect on Websites

Chapter 7

ADA Compliance and How it Affects Web Designers

In the quest for equality and fairness in accessing public and private information on the internet, the Department of Justice in America passed a law in 1990 that all information in websites should be accessed by all people. The core aim was very simple; allow maximum access of information by people with disabilities. Webmasters and web designers are commanded to ensure that their websites comply with set standards so that people can acquire information easily.

Web Designer Roles

Web Designers need to ensure that from the way documents are arranged, the graphic layout, software enhancements to font's sizes and colors should comply with ADA guidelines and should all be easily accessible by people with disabilities and normal people.

Making websites ADA compliant would help ensure and promote equality where all people would have equal chances of getting valuable information. A Key responsibility would be to ensure to work to or above WCAG 2.0 level AA guidelines in making the website to promote easy accessibility.
Web designers, especially the ones that cooperate with or receive funds from government entities should follow these guidelines.

Is There Help You Can Get as a Web Designer?

Nobody is a monopoly of wisdom and you don't wake up one day knowing everything, so if the issue of ADA compliance web design is not clear to you, you should seek help. You can choose to learn by being taught the skills or hire a professional for you. These professionals are going to design, implement and test accessibility of the website and it's pages until all tests confirm the website is ADA compliant.

They would produce a statement of accessibility, which can prove valuable if asked to defend actions in court.

When your website has accessibility certifications, everyone can access it and you have a stronger case if asked to defend your website of accused of violating the ADA law, indeed it would be harder for an accuser to get legal representation if the case looked harder to make, thanks to the compliant coding, test results and certificate to back it up.

How ADA Compliance Affects Your Web Designer Job?

No webmaster would like his or her website to be non-ADA compliant. The moment clients realize that you lack such a valuable skill you may find clients look to other alternatives. It is a skill worth learning and a real benefit to your clients, current and future; so book your classes so that you become a complete web designer expert.

Chapter 8

How and Why You Should Test Your Website for ADA Compliance

There are four principles that determine the accessibility of the website based on the American Disability Act. It needs to be perceivable, operable, understandable and robust. (22) When making your website perceivable, it means that your website needs to have an interface and information that is presentable in manner that they can recognize. In terms of being operable, people regardless of their limitation should be able to successfully operate the interface of your site. The content and the operation found in your website should also be within their capacity to understand. Finally, it also needs to be robust in order to be successfully interpreted by the assistive technology. (22) If you think your website falls under this category; it is time for ADA compliant website testing.

What is the American Disability Act? And It's Effect on Websites

How to Test a Website for ADA Compliance

A business owner needs to ensure that their website is ADA compliant. Those who do not may be missing out an opportunity to attract a new set of customers, and - as I am sure you have realized by now - can find themselves in a middle of a legal claim against them. But how do you make sure that your website is ADA compliance? ADA compliance website testing should be conducted by a website development company familiar in the various issues surrounding the ADA.

But if you want to know how to test a website for ADA compliance before you allow it to be tested by a website development company, you can test it yourself using online tools such as WAVE (18). Simply key in the URL of your website, and after a few moments, the online tool will be creating a report on the accessibility of your website.

The tool can be used for WCAG 2.0 A, WCAG 2.0 AA and Section 508 testing. The application will present the issues that it discovered in your website based on five categories.

1. **Errors** – these absolutely have to be the first priority, errors must be fixed. Examples include form fields with empty form labels.
2. **Alerts** – Notification of breaches of the rules that need to be addressed, but of a lower importance than Errors. An example could be a website not having a title instead of an H1 heading.
3. **Features** – Need to be addressed and are usually simple fixes. For example, images need to have Alt tags.
4. **Structural Elements** – these are errors flagged in the website code structure, for example using heading tags but not in sequential order.
5. **HTML5 and ARIA** – these are errors in the display of code that can affect how code reliant browsers understand see the webpage. For example a menu not identified in the code as being navigation code.

What is the American Disability Act? And It's Effect on Websites

Web designers are responsible in adding the ADA compliant features in the applications and the website. Through ADA compliance website testing, they will be able to understand the problems of our accessibility and make adjustments to make their work ADA compliant.

Chapter 9

What is Required to Ensure a Website is ADA Compliant

Creating a website for your business adds a tremendous amount of value, and it's definitely something that you want to take seriously. It's going to help you expand your reach, get new customers, target segmented and quality audience and much more. However, there are several things that you need to ensure in order to meet certain legislative requirements.

The tools introduced in this book will explain the specifics for your websites and give advice and solutions on an error by error basis.

What is the American Disability Act? And It's Effect on Websites

Things to Consider when Designing for ADA Compliance

When it comes to designing for ADA compliance, there are many factors you would need to take into account. The ADA refers to organizations and businesses with more than 15 employees. However, ensuring compliance is highly beneficial for all sorts of businesses which want to expand their reach and get to people with certain impairments. Here are some ADA web design tips that you might want to take into account

- All the images, video files as well as plug-ins and audio files need to have an alt tag.
- All the complex graphics are thoroughly accompanied by descriptions with detailed text.
- The alt descriptions must be particularly descriptive of the purpose of the said objects.
- You need to add closed captions to the videos.

- You need to add audio descriptions.
- You need to create a text transcript.
- Your page should provide alternative links to your own Image Map

Of course, these don't describe all the things that you need to take into account when it comes to designing for ADA compliance, but they should provide a good start for how you plan and map out your web design, and where to look for code and design improvements, to make them part f your routine work. Making them routine to your work is one good reason which you might want to make sure that you hire an outside specialist with experience in order for him/her/them to provide you with the necessary guidance and assistance, and systems to make sure it becomes part of the way you work, not an audit after the work is completed.

Chapter 10

ADA Compliance Testing and It's Importance

Testing a website for compliance is done to verify if the website fulfills the ADA rules. People with disabilities use assistive technology or devices to access information from the websites, which is why every page and public element needs to be tested if it works well with the used technology. In the event that your site is found to be incompetent, you would be needed to undergo the necessary enhancements so that it becomes as required.

The Process and Components of Website Testing

Testing should across the possible operating systems and browser combinations and consider your target audience, industry trends, and the current analytics. The device accessibility and flexibility would also be tested on different operating systems including MAC, IOS, and Android.

More on what is involved in this testing is given below.

Testing it With Screen Readers

Screen readers are assistive technology devices that convert virtual screen messages to audio messages which people could hear and interpret easily. Many blind people normally use this technology so your website would be tested. It works on desktops, laptops, tablets and mobile phones.

Screen Magnifiers

For people with low vision or people who are short sighted, magnifiers help them to make it easier to read and understand content on your website.

Magnifiers are options on browsers, and it's a simple test to check if your content is magnified when screen magnifiers are used.

Further Tests

The other tests include;

- Speech input recognition devices which help users to command the monitor and screen more easily.
- Alternative input devices; these allow people to use other devices like use a phone instead of a mouse to control the monitors or computer screens.
- Copy testing; ensuring the text is well written and easily to follow and understand.

Importance of Testing Compliance

ADA compliance website testing is the most logical way to find out if your website complying with the law. And compliance is essential because it means you serve all people fairly without discrimination.

Chapter 11

Why it's so important if you run A Business?

ADA compliance and business is important for the 1 in 5 Americans who have a disability. (19) It may take some time to make your business and website ADA compliant, but it is an important part of your business. Here are some reasons why you should become ADA compliant.

1. The Law

Above all, as you should have realized by now, it's the law. ADA compliance is your responsibility as a business owner. ADA is designed to protect people with disabilities and remove factors that create barriers, which make it impossible for them to get service. All businesses need to be ADA compliant. If you do not meet the guidelines in the ADA, you can have a complaint filed against your business. The fine can be large, and are not usually covered by business insurance.

What is the American Disability Act? And It's Effect on Websites

2. Helps You Build and Keep Your Customer

Around 1 in 5 Americans, today have a type of disability. (19) This a huge number and if you also count their friends, family and caregivers to the list of shoppers, who could all be possible customers for your business. There are estimates that over $3 trillion dollars is spent every year by people with disabilities and the people shopping with them. (23) Not being ADA complaint means that you are losing out on these sales. Online businesses have even more to lose because many people with disabilities shop online to avoid leaving their homes.

3. The Aging Population

ADA compliance for your website does not just benefit people with disabilities, but it also helps the aging population, with easier to read fonts, well defined structure and clear images and colors. This makes the website simpler to use and read for them.

Making your website accessible to people of all ages is becoming more important than ever.
Of note the elderly population, as a demographic, is growing quickly, and as age leads to deterioration of the body, can lead to disabilities as well.

4. Financial Assistance and Tax Write-Offs

The ADA helps businesses that want to be complaint with the guidelines that are set. There is financial assistance from the IRS called the Disabled Access Credit that can help your business cover the money to make your business accessible. Once your business is ADA compliant, you can file your taxes with that information. Depending on the size of your business, you can receive up to $5,000 every year that you are complaint. The maximum allowable credit each year is currently $5,000, or 50 percent of the first $10,000 past $250. This makes the changes that you need to make more affordable. (21)

What is the American Disability Act? And It's Effect on Websites

"wikiHow to Claim Disabled Access Credit" shows how to make this claim with step by step processes and links to the IRS documents.

http://www.wikihow.com/Claim-Disabled-Access-Credit

5. It Does Not Take a Lot of Money

Point 4 highlights there is government assistance for this, but it need not be an expensive affair in itself anyway.

Most times you just need to make simple changes. This can be an ongoing project, to help keep the costs down.

ADA compliance for websites is becoming an important partnership because disabilities are now common place. The extra time and money that you need to make your business ADA compliant can seem like it is not worth it on the face of it. However, being ADA compliant allows the 1 in 5 Americans to use your website and shop at your business. (19)

Chapter 12

ADA Compliance and how it Effects Your Charity and Charitable Business

Since a website would not be easily accessible by people with disabilities if not made to comply with ADA protocols, it would not be effective in the charitable business.

When your website is ADA compliant, it's a credential you can proudly show that demonstrates your belief in your ideals, and what you stand for.

How ADA compliance Affects Charity

When the website is not complaint, it runs the risk of legal action against it, and this likely would be well publicized as charities that do not provide a service for people with disabilities would by definition, be of interest to the media and the audience at large. It might scare away donors and well-wishers.

What is the American Disability Act? And It's Effect on Websites

Make sure that you are compliant to increase the charity from people.

ADA compliance charitable business would be enhanced through a perfectly built and tested website. Make the website compliant, touch the hearts of many people, get more donations and do wonderful things to the disabled. You can build for yourself and excellent reputation that will make you go globally and do great things, and if your charity has competition hat are not ADA compliant, it's another Unique Selling Point to win over business.

Let it Be Handled by Professionals

If you find it hard to make your charitable business compliant, there are experts who can ensure that your website follows all the set protocols so that you don't land in the wrong side of the law.

These professionals have the ability to start from designing to implementation of the website so that you get a compliant website that will function to serve all people equally. Make sure that your website gets tested for compliance and get certified so that you can operate without any risk of legal action being taken against you.

Professionals can also train you to do and manage this in house. If this interests you, use the tools in chapter four, to assess if it's something you are comfortable with taking on.

Chapter 13

Section 508 Compliance Examples With Fixes

Before we move on to discussing what are 508 compliance issues and how to properly get them fixed, it's important to understand what this standard stands for and why is it important to comply with it. The compliance standards which are set by the Section 508 of the Rehabilitation Act of 1973 require that federal agencies provide software and website which is accessible to people with different disabilities. This basically means that section 508 compliance requires your website to be properly accessible to all sorts of users, regardless of their disabilities. The rules set forth in the provisions are related to websites which are run by government agencies, public higher education institutions, federal-funded non-profit organizations and public K-12 schools. (13) Now that we've cleared this out let's move to the most common issues and how to fix them.

Common Section 508 Compliance Issues With Fixes
The Page has Markup Errors

This is a very common issue and in order to correct the issue one would have to use a validator tool. This is going to make sure that the substantial parsing errors are properly avoided.

Identify Row and Column Headers in the Tables of Data which Use TH Elements

In order to fix this particular issue, one would have to use header elements or other table mark-ups which are deemed appropriate in order to make the headers determinable by a program.

Use the LANG Attribute in Order to Be Able to Identify Page Language

In order to be able to fix this issue, you would have to identify the default language of a particular document. This is done by providing the LANG attribute on the HTML element.

What is the American Disability Act? And It's Effect on Websites

Of course, there are other issues which might arise that are compromising the section 508 compliance, but these are the most common. Section 508 compliance issues must be handled promptly in order to limit the negative impact that they are inevitably going to cause. The aforementioned tips should provide you with a helping hand.

Chapter 14

Conclusions

Whether you are a business owner, a charity or a web designer who servers clients in business or charity, it's important to understand and comply with the ADA regulations.

The immediate benefit is peace of mind that you have protected yourself from a possible lawsuit; but you have the additional benefit of helping your website to allow you to serve the 1 in 5 Americans who are disabled, and, depending on your business, people from outside the USA as well.

With the tools and advice given in this book, you can even test your website against the competition and discover how much of a competitive edge this can give you.

Start by take a few moments to test your website, find out what is required and get yourself compliant.

What is the American Disability Act? And It's Effect on Websites

For more help and to get a free website audit with advice on what's required, visit www.compliant.website
http://compliant.website/request-a-free-web-page-audit/

References

(1) WCAG 2.0 AA Gains Prominence as Website Accessibility Standard

Friday, January 13, 2017

http://www.natlawreview.com/article/wcag-20-aa-gains-prominence-website-accessibility-standard

(2) Internet Accessibility Policy May 5th, 2011

https://cio.gov/internet-accessibility-policy/

(3) Legal update - February 2016 February 2016,

http://businessdisabilityforum.org.uk/media-centre/newsletter/legal-update/legal-february-2016/

(4) Monster.com First in Industry to Make Website Accessible for Blind Users January 30, 2013,

http://www.mass.gov/ago/news-and-updates/press-releases/2013/2013-01-30-monster-agreement.html

(5) Website Accessibility Checklist July 14, 2016

http://compliant.website/website-accessibility-checklist/

(6) Request a Free Web Page Audit, July 21st, 2016

http://compliant.website/request-a-free-web-page-audit/

What is the American Disability Act? And It's Effect on Websites

(7) The Americans With Disabilities Act of 1990

https://www.eeoc.gov/eeoc/history/35th/1990s/ada.html

(8) Frequently Asked Questions, January 14th, 2017

https://www.disabilitystatistics.org/faq.cfm#Q9

(9) Website Accessibility: Department of Justice's Filings in Lawsuits Give Warnings, July 21, 2015,

https://www.iaml.com/blog/website-accessibility-department-justice%E2%80%99s-filings-lawsuits-give-warnings

(10) Americans with Disabilities Act Questions and Answers, February 2001,

https://www.ada.gov/qandaeng.htm

(11) More Businesses Face Lawsuits Challenging Website Accessibility March 17th, 2016

http://www.lexology.com/library/detail.aspx?g=aba1fd8a-a1a4-4bdd-a5de-ad98a6fb19eb

(12) The Wave of Website and Other ADA Accessibility Claims – What You Should Know, February 22nd 2016 https://www.littler.com/publication-press/publication/wave-website-and-other-ada-accessibility-claims-%E2%80%93-what-you-should-know

(13) Section 508 Law, August 7, 1998, https://www.section508.gov/section508-laws

(14) Voluntary Product Accessibility Template (VPAT) Policy & Information, June 1st, 2015, https://www.state.gov/documents/organization/126552.pdf

(15) How to File an ADA Complaint with the U.S. Department of Justice, https://www.ada.gov/filing_complaint.htm

(16) Visual impairment and blindness, August 2014, http://www.who.int/mediacentre/factsheets/fs282/en/

(17) What is Web Accessibility for Websites?, 24th June 2016, http://compliant.website/web-accessibility-websites/

(18) Desktop Browser Version Market Share, December 2016, https://www.netmarketshare.com/browser-market-share.aspx?qprid=2&qpcustomd=0

What is the American Disability Act? And It's Effect on Websites

(19) Web Accessibility Evaluation Tool

http://wave.webaim.org/

(20) Nearly 1 in 5 People Have a Disability in the U.S., Census Bureau Reports, July 25, 2012, https://www.census.gov/newsroom/releases/archives/miscellaneous/cb12-134.html

(21) wikiHow to Claim Disabled Access Credit, March 2016, http://www.wikihow.com/Claim-Disabled-Access-Credit

(22) Understanding the Four Principles of Accessibility

https://www.w3.org/TR/UNDERSTANDING-WCAG20/intro.html

(23) Reframing Disability (PowerPoint Presentation)

https://www.missouristate.edu/assets/disability/reframing_disability.pptx

About the Author

Scott Whitehead has been designing and building websites for over 20 years, and is a recognized expert in web design and marketing.

He served as Professor of Digital Marketing to MBA Students at Groupe INSEEC and has won several web design awards for his work for clients across the globe.

His business Advance Further LLC in Las Vegas, Nevada assists businesses across the USA to get their websites working effectively and compliant with the ADA legislation. Outside of work, Scott enjoys music and watching the NFL.

More details about Scott and his work, including tools to help you get your website compliant can be found at Compliant.Website.

T: 702 997 2344

E: hello@compliant.website

www.ingramcontent.com/pod-product-compliance
Lightning Source LLC
Chambersburg PA
CBHW061220180526
45170CB00003B/1084